# No
# Greater
# Love

*No Greater Love*, alongside the author's earlier study called *God's Foolishness*, offers what could almost be seen as a potted history of spirituality, readable and relevant to all people of faith. Brian Gallagher finds his own experience of God echoed in spiritual writers as early as the fourth century and in a number of other contemporary writers. He says that all of these authors have influenced his own spirituality. Brian concludes that only when we have experienced God's love, God's gift of Godself, are we able to live truly contented lives, even through the inevitable ups and downs of life. What emerges from the teachings of the women and men studied in this book is that our knowing God's love and our love of God in response, like our desire for God, does not always involve feeling, let alone warm cosy feeling. Love deepens relationship, even when accompanied by painful feelings – or no feelings. I highly recommend Brian Gallagher's work.

SUE RICHARDSON PBVM,
*retired Vicar for Religious, Archdiocese of Melbourne.*

This book is a finely composed collection of spiritual writers who have shaped and nourished the rich tradition of spiritual life. It also reveals the unitive space where the centuries old human encounters with God's self-emptying love meet and embrace, uphold and penetrate one another. One significant characteristic of such human encounter with God's love that Brian points out for us is that it is very obscure and unknown, as though one is walking in the dark. In other words, in this encounter with God's indescribable and immeasurable love, we are not in control. It is pure grace of God that painfully and amazingly purifies and transforms us from our attachments and compulsions, whether conscious or unconscious. Once we know this in our inner life, everything else falls into place.

KHOI DOAN NGUYEN MSC,
author of *A Quiet Place Within.*

In these simple yet profound reflections, Brian distils a lifetime of prayer and reflection as he teases out the essence of our human experience of God. He writes as his subjects wrote, from an ongoing desire to know the full freedom of Love. He describes the incessant drawing of Love for all souls regardless of how they experience or imagine that they don't experience this Love. And he has a knack for writing just enough to whet the appetite for a fuller understanding, and yet leave the reader with enough freedom to explore the concepts in terms of their own life. Brian's reflections help us to see that we are set free to live life to the full only with, through and in this marvellous Love of God. To paraphrase a quote from John of the Cross, in praying this volume, we might find that *so tenderly God's love becomes our own.*

MICHELLE VASS,
*Director St Mary's Towers Retreat Centre, Douglas Park, NSW.*

The Human
Experience of God

# No
# Greater
# Love

Brian Gallagher msc

COVENTRY
PRESS

Published in Australia by
Coventry Press
33 Scoresby Road
Bayswater VIC 3153

ISBN 9780648982289

Catalogue-in-Publication entry is available from the National Library of Australia http://catalogue.nla.gov.au

Cover design by Ian James – www.jgd.com.au
Text design by Coventry Press
Set in Fontin 11pt

Printed in Australia

# Table of Contents

# Introduction

This book is a sequel to my earlier book called *God's Foolishness*. In that book, I honoured several women and men who had influenced me over the years, people whose lives and writings had challenged me, encouraged me and inspired me. The common thread through their writings was that human wisdom would have judged that these women and men had little to offer. Yet, all stand as evidence that God's foolishness is far wiser than human wisdom.

The choice of writers in this book is based on the same desire to recognise people who have been major influences in my life and my spirituality. I now add another dozen people to the eight I had discussed in *God's Foolishness*. The choice from others who could well have been included was quite arbitrary: they are all names that roll off my tongue easily and often. After naming this group of women and men, I notice that all but three are ordained clergy, one a bishop. Over half are monks; indeed there are three abbots. The exceptions are the women – one a nun in an enclosed contemplative community, the other an anchoress, a hermit living a life of prayer and asceticism – and Gerald May, a happily married man.

Though I admit to some surprise when I first realised this, the prominence of clerics is understandable from an historical perspective. We know that for centuries, in society at large, women were denied any formal education. In church, the sad reality is that women were forbidden to write and publish, and lay men, if not forbidden, were given little encouragement. Until quite recent times, the history of spirituality includes very few lay women and men. As a result, spirituality appeared to be the realm of professional Church men, priests and monks. They were the ones who wrote and, for the most part, the ones who read the writings. Hopefully, the readership of this book will be much wider.

On a more personal level, these *are* the people whose writings have inspired me. I can still remember my delight, indeed my excitement, when I first read the sentence at the head of each chapter. I was immediately drawn into reading further. But I knew already that God's Spirit was inviting me to some newness – in my own prayer, in my ongoing reflection, and in my subsequent writing. I write for the same reason as the people I write about wrote: my hope that others will find inspiration and encouragement in their faith. To paraphrase Jesus' words, 'I received without payment, I now give without payment' (Matthew 10:8). If there is any theme to the writings of this group of people, I believe that it is the experience of God in their own lives. All of them knew God's personal love, God's gift of Godself, beyond question. 'God's love has been poured into our hearts through the Holy Spirit that has been given to us.' (Romans 5:5) Some experienced this love in their intense longing for God, others in times of intimate closeness to God, others still in their deep trust in times of struggle and uncertainty in their life.

Karl Rahner and Denis Edwards have coined the term 'God's self-bestowal' to describe this gift of God's love – another source of excitement for me when I first heard the term. God is self-giving love. God gives Godself to us in creation, in incarnation and the life of grace, and in final fulfillment. Indeed, there is 'no greater love' (John 15:13).

How each of us experiences this gift of God's love – and responds to it – will be unique to us, as it was for the people whose lives and teachings I now reflect on. I pray that we may all know this personal love of God in our lives.

# Human Desire for God

*His heart, insofar as it burned with a holy desire
for God, was assuredly a place of God already.*

WILLIAM OF ST THIERRY, JULIAN OF NORWICH,
GREGORY OF NYSSA, THOMAS MERTON

Bill Connolly was my supervisor when I was preparing for my
ministry in spiritual direction in Boston close to fifty years
ago. Bill was my teacher, mentor, guide for twelve months.
We became good friends.

I would call Bill an 'untypical' Jesuit, close to 'unlikely'.
In my experience, many Jesuit spiritual directors base their
approach on St Ignatius' *Spiritual Exercises*. Not Bill. The
only time I recall his mentioning Ignatius was when he
asked me to direct a 30-day retreat without mentioning
the name 'Ignatius' or the words 'Spiritual Exercises'! He
was emphasising the need to work only with whatever was
happening in the retreatant's life and prayer, not with any
predetermined plan or expectation. In fact, Bill was quite
eclectic in his reading and his teaching. He introduced me
to many of the classical writers in spirituality, from Gregory
of Nyssa and Augustine (century 4), through the medieval
writers and the 'Golden Age' in spiritual writing (centuries
15 and 16) to those closer to home, as John Chapman and
Thomas Keating (century 20) – all mentioned in this book.

A favourite was **William of St Thierry**, a twelfth century monk, who wrote an *Exposition on the Song of Songs*, amongst many other works. The Bible's book called *The Song of Songs* celebrates a lover's longing and searching for her beloved, interpreted by William and other Christian writers to refer to our longing and searching for God. God's presence seems elusive. God seems to come – 'Look, he comes, leaping upon the mountains, bounding over the hills' (Song 2:8) – and to disappear just as quickly – 'upon my bed at night, I sought him whom my soul loves. I sought him, but found him not. I called him but he gave no answer' (3:1, 5:6). The lover alternates between sheer delight in the beloved's presence – 'I am my beloved's and my beloved is mine.' (6:3) – and desperate longing for the beloved's return – 'Return, return, my loved one' (6:13).

Flowing from his reflection and his prayer with the scripture, William taught:

> The soul begins to understand by experience the mysteries of Divine Love: that if he withdraws from her so often, it is to make her seek him more ardently; and if he sometimes surrenders himself to her who loves him, it is to prevent her from being engrossed in excessive sadness.[1]

It makes good sense to me that we learn this from our experience. I know that those times when God seems very close and I rejoice in God's consoling gift, those times do not last. Indeed, it seems to me that they are always short-lived. Later spiritual writers, Teresa of Avila for example, believed

---

[1] William of St Thierry, *Exposition on the Song of Songs* (Cistercian Series, Ireland, 1970), volume 2, #166.

that such glimpses of God's presence were not only enough to sustain us, but that their short-life was evidence that they were genuine gifts of God. We ourselves cannot create an experience of God, and we cannot cling to it when it is given. When the gift is given, it serves to whet the appetite: we long for more. William returned to this theme throughout his exposition, praying 'O that your comings and your goings might be more frequent', and calling on Psalm 42:7 – 'deep calls on deep'.

He went further – this is what captured my imagination, sitting at Bill Connolly's feet. William taught that what seems to us like God's absence, in fact, is really a different experience of God. Our very longing for God in those times of 'absence' is itself a gift of God. Our very longing is an experience of God. Hence the quotation at the head of the chapter:

His heart insofar as it burned with a holy desire for God, was assuredly a place of God already.[2]

This is William of St Thierry's lasting teaching. Later, I discovered the same teaching in several other writers. It is the Christian tradition.

For example, from **Augustine's** *Confessions*:

You made us for yourself and our hearts are restless till they rest in you.[3]

I have learned to love you late, Beauty ever ancient and ever new. I have learned to love you late. You were within me,

---

[2] *Exposition on the Song of Songs*, #76.
[3] Augustine, *Confessions* (Penguin, 1961), Book I.

and I was in the world, outside of myself. I searched for you outside myself. You were within me, but I was not with you.[4]

From **Julian of Norwich**'s *Revelations of Divine Love*:

I saw him and I sought him. I had him and I wanted him. God is our true resting place. God wants it to be known that God's goodness encloses us. For we are his own. It is God's Spirit which gives life for us to grow in grace. And we can never stop this longing until we see God's loving face.[5]

Our longing for God is never fully satisfied. Both our desire for God and our awareness that any experience of God still falls short are gifts of God. The earliest record of this teaching is found in **Gregory of Nyssa**, Bishop of Caesarea in century 4. In his *Life of Moses*, Gregory reflects on texts from the book of Exodus where Moses is said to have seen God 'face to face'.

Speaking of Moses:

He shone with glory. And although lifted up through such lofty experiences, he is still unsatisfied in his desire for more. He still thirsts for that with which he constantly filled himself to capacity, and he asks to attain as if he had never partaken, beseeching God to appear to him...[6]

---

[4] *Confessions*, Book X.
[5] Julian of Norwich, *Revelations of Divine Love* (Penguin, 1966), Second revelation.
[6] Gregory of Nyssa, *The Life of Moses*, Classics of Western Spirituality (NY: Paulist Press, 1978), #230.

Gregory summarised his teaching in this sentence:

> This truly is the vision of God: never to be satisfied in the desire to see him.[7]

The challenge for me, maybe for all of us, is to be satisfied with our unsatisfied longing for God, to trust that God is truly present in what seems like God's absence. I am encouraged by Julian of Norwich who heard these words from God in another of her revelations:

> Pray inwardly though you find no joy in it. For it does good, though you feel nothing, see nothing, yes even though you think you cannot pray. For when you are dry and empty, sick and weak, your prayers please me – though there be little enough to please you. All believing prayer is precious to me.

Much later, **Thomas Merton** (century 20) expressed the same conviction:

> The absence of activity is only apparent. Below the surface, the mind and will are drawn into the orbit of an activity that is deep and intense and supernatural, and which overflows into our whole being and brings forth incalculable fruits.[8]

The trust in God that such 'dry and empty' prayer calls for is a theme that will recur in what follows.

---

[7] *The Life of Moses*, #239.
[8] Thomas Merton, *Seeds of Contemplation* (Wheathampstead, Hertfordshire: Anthony Clarke Books, 1961), 188.

# The Gift of Love

*Your grace, your glory, fills me so
tenderly, your love becomes my own.*

MARJORIE FLOWER, JOHN OF THE CROSS, FRANCIS DE SALES

Marjorie Flower is an Australian Carmelite Sister in the Carmel community in Port Moresby. Her one publication called *Centered on Love* is her beautiful translation of the poems of St John of the Cross.[9]

Over a number of years, I had read and taught John's works, particularly his description and recommendations around the experience of 'dark night', discussed in the following chapter. But I think I was always a little tentative about John of the Cross, imagining maybe that he was too negative, too ascetic. I realise now how easily John of the Cross' teaching can be misunderstood.

It is true that John of the Cross wrote some sentences that seem almost bizarre, beyond belief, on first reading. For example:

---

[9] John of the Cross, *Centered on Love: the Poems of St John of the Cross* translated by Marjorie Flower OCD. (Varroville NSW: Carmelite Nuns, 1983, reprinted 2002).

To reach satisfaction in all, desire its possession in nothing.
To come to possess all,
desire the possession of nothing.[10]

We are dealing with the denudation of the soul's
appetites and gratifications. This is what leaves it
free and empty of all things, even though it
possesses them.[11]

Allow the soul to remain in rest and quietude, even though it
may seem very obvious... that they are
doing nothing and wasting time...[12]

I have found that a study of John's poetry gives these statements their context.

Several translations of John of the Cross' poetry are available. In Marjorie Flower's 'Translator's Notes', she speaks of the difficulty involved in translating poetry; she says even more so for the poetry of John of the Cross, whose 'words are almost unbearably rich and allusive'. In the outcome, 'the equivalent English words rarely have any relation to the magical quality of the Spanish words he uses so effectively'. I'm grateful that Marjorie Flower persevered, nonetheless. She knows John well and, in my reading, identifies with much of John's experience. Her work 'springs from a long friendship with Juan de la Crux'. In what follows, I name several examples of Flower's translation that clarify John's experience for me, where other previous translations did not.

---

[10] *The Ascent of Mount Carmel* in *The Collected Works of St John of the Cross*, edited by Kieran Kavanaugh and Otilio Rodriguez (Washington, DC: Institute of Carmelite Studies, 1973), Book I, chapter 13.
[11] *The Ascent of Mount Carmel*, Book I, chapter 3.
[12] *The Dark Night*. Book I, chapter 10.4.

We know that John had a profoundly intimate, loving experience of God when in prison in 1577. It was in that dark dungeon, deprived of any reading or writing, that John composed and memorised his first poem, *The Spiritual Canticle*.[13] He wrote the poem later. This verse captures his experience:

> You looked with love upon me
> and deep within, your eyes imprinted grace.
> This mercy set me free
> held in your love's embrace
> to lift, my eyes adoring to your face.

Much later, John wrote that 'the delicateness of delight felt in this contact is inexpressible.'[14] Indeed, poetry became the best possible expression. John's poem, *The Dark Night*, came soon after. 'Dark night' may have been a reference to his months in prison or may be seen as a symbol of his experience. In darkness, hidden, with 'no one to see my flight, and no other guide or light, save one that in my heart burned bright as day', John is led to his Beloved. 'Ah', says John, 'the sheer grace'.

Flower's sentence 'this mercy set me free' is not found in other translations. The translation in *The Collected Works of St John of the Cross*, for example, is:

> For this you loved me ardently. And thus my eyes deserved to adore what they beheld in you.[15]

---

[13] *Centered on Love*, 14-21.
[14] *The Living Flame of Love*. Stanza 2.21.
[15] *The Collected Works of St John of the Cross*, 715.

Rather than my deserving to adore God, Flower's translation highlights the gift of God's love, setting me free to adore God. As I discuss below, the experience of God's love setting us free is central to the teaching of John of the Cross. The experience of dark night is exactly that: God's love frees us from anything that might hold us back from God. Marjorie Flower clearly knows this.

Here is another example. Some years later, John wrote *The Living Flame*.[16] One can imagine John still trying to express his experience of God:

Ah! Gentle and so loving
you wake within me, proving
that you are there in secret and alone;
Your fragrant breathing stills me,
your grace, your glory fills me
so tenderly your love becomes my own.

Once again, the final line 'your love becomes my own' is not found in other translations. The translation that I cited above in *The Collected Works of St John of the Cross* says 'how tenderly you swell my heart with love', which seems to me to miss John's meaning. Rather, 'your love becomes my own' captures not only that we love because we know we are loved, but also that our loving is to share in God's love. We are privileged to bring God's love into our world. I note, too, how 'tenderly' God works in us – a favourite word for John of the Cross.

---

[16] *Centered on Love*, 22.

Clearly, John's teaching is based on his personal experience. When we approach God in love – and know God's love – he believes that we are gradually liberated, freed of any attachment to anything other than God. Moreover, we are freed of any need to *feel* God's presence: as he wrote in the earlier quotations, we don't even desire such satisfaction. Our love and our desire are focused solely on God, not the gifts of God: we are content to leave all to God in faith.

As in the earlier writing of Gregory of Nyssa and William of St Thierry, John says that, even in our love and desire for God, we may feel 'nothing' at all. Love does not depend on feeling. At that point, John says that the temptation for many people, feeling nothing, is to imagine that they have regressed in their relationship with God. Some people, I know, resolve to do more – to give more time to prayer, to concentrate more – as though to recover some felt closeness to God. In fact, we are being 'set free', as he prayed.

John is well aware that this freedom does not come suddenly, as though once and for all. In the same poem *The Living Flame*, John still prays to be set free:

Flame alive, compelling,
yet tender past all telling,
reaching the secret centre of my soul.
Since now evasion's over,
finish your work, my Lover,
break the last thread, wound me and make me whole!

Flower's translation of *The Living Flame* also has quite a different emphasis from earlier translations. 'Since now, evasion's over' contrasts with 'now you are not oppressive' in the earlier translation. My experience suggests that, if there is any barrier to my receiving God's gift of love, the barrier is my evasion – Marjorie Flower's word – not God's holding back. I believe this, too, is true to the teaching of John of the Cross.

John's teaching would be quite hollow without that initial loving experience of God. God's love sets us free. In that freedom, John of the Cross encourages loving and peaceful attentiveness to God.[17] In *The Spiritual Canticle* above, he says simply, we adore God. 'Adore' may be a rather old-fashioned word, but it captures well the basic Christian stance before God, the giver of all good things.

Other writers speak of the same 'loving and peaceful attentiveness to God' that is John's encouragement. One notable example is found in **Francis de Sales**, Bishop of Geneva in century 17. Francis shares the gift of words with Marjorie Flower: in his book *Treatise on Divine Love*, he uses the image of a baby at her mother's breast to capture loving attentiveness:

> You see the child hold and press the breast with its mouth, making soft sounds all the while... (finally) you see the child very softly close its little eyes and little by little give way to sleep. Still, it does not release the breast, on which it exerts no action but a slow and almost insensible movement of the lips whereby it draws in milk that it swallows imperceptibly. It does this without thinking, but surely not without pleasure. If the breast is withdrawn before the child falls sound asleep, it wakes up and cries bitterly. Thus, by the distress it has at such privation, it testifies how great was

---

[17] John of the Cross, *The Dark Night*, Book I, chapter 10.

the pleasure of possession. It is the same with the soul that is in repose and quiet before God.[18]

Echoing William of St Thierry, Julian of Norwich, and Thomas Merton earlier, Francis also wrote:

There are times when the soul neither hears its beloved nor speaks to him, nor does it feel any sign of his presence. It simply knows that it is in God's presence, to whom it is pleasing that the soul is there.[19]

Interestingly, Francis wrote two books of spirituality. In the first, *An Introduction to the Devout Life*, he spoke of the recommended practices to help the development of a 'devout life'. I imagine such encouragement to acts of charity, regular meditation, confession, examination of conscience would have been the accepted practices of the time. Nine years later, Francis wrote *On the Love of God* with an entirely different emphasis. Acknowledging that he was writing only 'what he had learned' (from his spiritual direction, primarily of Jane Frances de Chantal, a Visitation nun in the local convent), Francis wrote this time about how God works in a person's life, not what we do or should be doing.

Francis now focused on the gift of God's love, as did John of the Cross. Also paralleling John of the Cross, Francis taught the importance of setting our desire on God, not on the gifts of God, the virtue he named 'indifference':

---

[18] Francis de Sales, *On the Love of God* (Garden City, NY: Doubleday & Co., 1963), Book 6, chapter 9.
[19] *On the Love of God*, Book 6, chapter 11.

If I like only pure water, what difference does it matter to me whether it is served in a goblet of gold or one of glass, since in either case I drink only the water? ... What does it matter whether God's will is offered to me in tribulation or in consolation?[20]

Focusing now on God's gift of love, Francis' writing turned to meditation and contemplation: 'We meditate to awaken love, we contemplate because we love.' He could well have added that we love because we know we are loved. His first book was more on meditation, the second *On the Love of God* included his teaching on contemplation. For Francis de Sales, the image of the baby at her mother's breast describes contemplation.

In the following chapter, I discuss John of the Cross' teaching on 'dark night' to explain how God, in fact, does set us free, in love – how God liberates us, to use John's earlier expression.

---

[20] *On the Love of God*, Book 9, Chapter 4.

# The Grace of Dark Night

*Be content with a loving and peaceful attentiveness to God.*

JOHN OF THE CROSS, JOHN CHAPMAN

John of the Cross, a Carmelite friar in century 16, is probably best known through his teaching on what he called the experience of 'dark night'. The core of this teaching is loving desire for God, clearly connecting him with earlier writers. Our desire for God, which we see as an experience of God, permeates all of our religious experience. Desire for God persists whether we are enjoying God's consolation or finding ourselves struggling with what seems like God's absence, highlighted above by Francis de Sales' image of our desire for pure water.

In the former instance – in God's consolation – William of St Thierry reminded us that even when we do experience God we are not satisfied, we long for more: our desire deepens. In the latter case – when God seems absent – we recall Jesus' words on the cross 'My God, my God, why have you forsaken me?' Even in that time of felt aloneness, Jesus then prayed 'Father, into your hands, I commend my spirit.' Jesus trusted himself to a God whom he felt had abandoned him. Such was his faith and his desire for God. This may well have been the inspiration for John of the Cross' understanding of his own experience.

John writes from his own experience, expressing that experience in advice and recommendations for others. In his book *Dark Night*, a commentary on his earlier poem with the same title, John writes initially about the experience of those he calls 'beginners' in their faith commitment. He notes what he considers to be fairly universal experience:

> It is at the time when they are going about their spiritual exercises with delight and satisfaction, when in their opinion the sun of divine favour is shining most brightly on them, that God darkens all this light and closes the door and spring of the sweet spiritual water they were tasting as often and as long as they desired... God now leaves them in such darkness that they do not know which way to turn in their discursive imaginings... God leaves them in such dryness that they not only fail to receive satisfaction and pleasure from their spiritual exercises and works, as they formerly did, but also find these exercises distasteful and bitter.[21]

In contemporary language, John is speaking of everyday people of faith, interested in and committed to following their beliefs. Their 'spiritual exercises' might include time given to prayer and reflection on life, attendance at liturgical celebrations, and care for other people. When these people pray, most commonly they use books of prayer or they adopt what traditionally is called 'meditation', reflecting on life and maybe on Sacred Scripture. This is what John calls a 'discursive' way of prayer. Such prayer is time well spent, often ending with some application to their everyday living.

---

[21] *The Dark Night*, Book I, chapter 8.

But we know from experience that after some time, such reflective prayer loses its attraction. It doesn't seem to satisfy as it used to. There is little consolation. John's description of this time is painted quite vividly with such evocative terminology as darkness, dryness, distasteful and bitter – words that Marjorie Flower calls 'unbearably rich and allusive'. We may choose different language to describe our personal experience, but I know from my long years as a spiritual director that something of this experience is common, maybe even to be expected if we are serious about our spiritual lives. This is the experience that John calls 'dark night'. He says it is a 'dark' time, not in any sinister sense, but in the sense that it is an experience that is difficult to understand – as though we cannot see where we are heading in the darkness.

John teaches that this is a time for trust, for faith in God's ever-presence. He says that a person who is in such darkness should not try to recover what used to be, and certainly should not force oneself to keep meditating. Rather, God is inviting deeper love and deeper trust – and patience. He writes:

> They should allow the soul to remain in rest and quietude, even though it may seem very obvious to them that they are doing nothing and wasting time... through patience and perseverance in prayer, they will be doing a great deal without activity on their part... They must be content simply with a loving and peaceful attentiveness to God, and live without the concern, without the effort, and without the desire to taste or feel him.
>
> If they know how to remain quiet, without care or solicitude about any interior or exterior work, they will soon in that

unconcern and idleness delicately experience the interior nourishment. This refection is so delicate that usually if the soul desires to tries to experience it, it cannot.[22]

John acknowledges the possibility that experiences of darkness and dryness might have some other cause – as examples, he mentions sin, disinterest, even sickness. And so, John gives three signs to be sure that one's experience is indeed God's work. The simplest expression of these signs is:

I cannot pray as I used to / I do not want an alternative / I do want God.[23]

John says that all three signs coexist in the dark night. But that 'I do want God' seems to me to permeate all: I want love, goodness, truth. It is this desire for God, in fact, that enables a person to persevere in dark night. And our desire for God is the surest indication that this time is gift of God. Indeed, as William of St Thierry taught, our desire for God is already to know God.

Painful as it might be for many of us – not only in our prayer, but also in what John referred to as our 'works' – this is a time of grace, of growth in our relationship with God. As I mentioned in the previous chapter, reflecting on John's poem *The Living Flame*, this is a time when we are being set free from inner attachments that we didn't even know we had, maybe from false images of God that we have learned earlier in life.

---

[22] *The Dark Night*, Book I, chapters 9 & 10.
[23] Iain Matthew, *The Impact of God* (London: Hodder & Stoughton, 1995), 148.

John calls this process 'purgation', another example of his vivid language. We are purged even of unconscious areas of our make-up that could hold back the development of our relationship with God. As I discuss in a later chapter, these are our *unfreedoms*, the areas of our inner life that are compulsive and which lead to behavioural habits contrary to our values. Other translations use the term 'purification', rather than 'purgation'. Either way, we remember that God works 'tenderly' to set us free.

As we are set free, accepting that it may be a slow gradual process, our approach to life changes. Life becomes simpler, less pressured and demanding, more open to God's everyday surprises. And our prayer changes: we find that we are more able to rejoice in God's presence, content with 'loving and peaceful attentiveness to God', as John wrote. This is contemplative prayer:

> In this state of contemplation... it is God who works in (the soul) ... At this time, a person's own efforts are of no avail... Those who are in this situation should feel comforted. They should persevere patiently and not be afflicted. Let them trust in God, who does not fail those who seek him with a simple and righteous heart.[24]

Reinforcing his experience that our own efforts are of no avail in our quest for God, John wrote elsewhere that 'nothing which could possibly be imagined or comprehended in this life can be a proximate means of union with God'.[25] John recalls God's word to Moses: 'you cannot see my face, for

---

[24] *The Dark Night*, Book I, chapters 9 & 10.
[25] *The Ascent of Mount Carmel*, Book II, chapter 8.

no one shall see me and live' (Exodus 33:20). Instead, we are invited to trust God as we are led through the dark night: as John has said, patience and perseverance are the order of the day.

Many other writers have cited, even expanded, John's teaching on the experience of dark night. For example, four centuries later, **John Chapman**, Abbot of Downside Abbey in the English Benedictine community, taught the very same experience. Chapman did not use the same terminology and did not mention John of the Cross by name. He may or may not have been influenced by John of the Cross. If he were not, it seems to me that his own independent experience serves to affirm John's. For today's readers, and certainly for the people for whom Chapman was writing, his language is more contemporary and more succinct.

Chapman's 'teaching' is found in his extensive correspondence with the people who wrote to him asking his guidance. The letters are published in his only book, *Spiritual Letters*.[26] Thankfully, Chapman added an Appendix in which he outlines fully his experience and his understanding of contemplative prayer.

John of the Cross encouraged loving attentiveness to God in times of dryness and darkness, the times when it seems like nothing is happening in one's prayer. Chapman's encouragement is his assurance that dry prayer is quite normal:

---

[26] John Chapman, *Spiritual Letters* (London: Sheed and Ward, 1935).

One must do it for God's sake. But one will not get any satisfaction out of it, in the sense of feeling 'I am good at prayer', or 'I have an infallible method'. That would be disastrous, since what we want to learn is precisely our own weakness, powerlessness, unworthiness... And one should wish for no prayer except precisely the prayer that God gives us – probably very distracted and unsatisfactory in every way.[27]

Admittedly, this is tough encouragement, repeated in Chapman's appendix:

The time of prayer is spent in the act of wanting God. It is an idiotic state, and feels like the completest waste of time... The strangest phenomenon is when we begin to wonder whether we mean anything at all, and if we are addressing anyone... Even the word God seems to mean nothing.[28]

This was followed immediately by the sentence: 'if we feel this curious and paradoxical condition, we are on the right road.' In other words, persevere, as John of the Cross recommended. As we have seen above, other writers have added that one is already experiencing God when 'the time of prayer is spent in the act of wanting God.' Maybe Chapman preferred tough encouragement. Either way, we are encouraged.

---

[27] *Spiritual Letters*, 52-53.
[28] *Spiritual Letters*, Appendix.

# God's Self-bestowal

*Creation is a Trinitarian act of Self-bestowal.*

DENIS EDWARDS, KARL RAHNER, YVES CONGAR

Denis Edwards was an Australian theologian, based in an Adelaide parish until his premature death in 2019. His theology of the Spirit, found in his books *Breath of Life*[29] and *How God Acts*[30] gave him international standing. Those books were followed by several works of ecological theology, Edwards' passion in later years. Much of Edwards' work flowed from his study of Karl Rahner.

Jesuit priest **Karl Rahner** is pre-eminent amongst theologians (century 20). Based at the university of Innsbruck, and later at Munich, Rahner wrote extensively throughout his career, culminating in his 23 volume *Theological Investigations*. Rahner died in 1984.

Rahner saw God as a self-giving God. This is who God is. A central insight in his theology is that God's action in creation, in incarnation and in the life of grace is the one act

---

[29] Denis Edwards, *Breath of Life: A Theology of the Creator Spirit* (Maryknoll, NY: Orbis Books, 2004).

[30] Denis Edwards, *How God Acts: Creation, Redemption and Special Divine Action* (Hindmarsh, SA: ATF Theology, 2010).

of God, grounded in the unity of the divine being.[31] From the beginning, God creates a world in which the Word is made flesh and the Spirit is poured out. The incarnation does not come about as a remedy for sin, as some theologies claim, but is central to God's creative act. The sending of the Spirit, often associated only with Pentecost, is also central to God's creative act.[32] All are gifts of God's very self. This loving gift of Godself, Rahner calls 'God's self-bestowal'.

Following Rahner, Edwards wrote that God's action in creation is 'a Trinitarian act of self-bestowal.' More fully:

> God chooses to give God's self in love to what is not divine, and so creation comes to be... the central insight of Christian revelation is that God gives God's self to us in the Word made flesh and in the Spirit poured out. This self-giving can be understood as defining every aspect of God's action in creation, redemption, and final fulfilment.[33]

Edwards' writing on the Holy Spirit developed from this understanding.

In Sacred Scripture, the Holy Spirit is revealed as *Ruah*, the breath of God breathing life into all creation (Genesis 1:2, 2:7). The Scriptures depict the Spirit as ever-present and all-pervading: 'Your immortal Spirit is in all things.' (Wisdom 12:1). 'Where can I go from your Spirit?' (Psalm 139:7) God's gift of the Spirit is present and sustains all life from the beginning of creation.

---

[31] *How God Acts*, 39-42.

[32] I develop this teaching in my book *Set me Free: Spiritual Direction and Discernment of Spirits* (Bayswater, Vic: Coventry Press, 2019), 23.

[33] *How God Acts*, 39-40.

Writing in dialogue with emerging cosmological discoveries, Edwards wrote:

> The history of the Spirit... is coexistent with the total life of the universe. God's Spirit has been breathing life into the processes of the evolving universe from the very first... the Spirit was present in the very emergence of the human, embracing early humans in self-offering love.[34]

Edwards is supported by **Yves Congar** who wrote a major tome on a theology of the Holy Spirit:

> The Spirit who is both one and transcendent is able to penetrate all things without violating or doing violence to them... The Spirit is unique and present everywhere, transcendent and inside all things, subtle and sovereign, able to respect freedom and to inspire it. The Spirit can further God's plan...[35]

That the gift of God's Spirit breathes in all creation – and has from the very beginning – is foundational in my understanding of the Spirit. It has several implications.

The first, taken from Edwards' writings is that this gift of Godself to creation implies a communion lived in all people and in all creation:

> If divine being is communion, then created being too exists only in and from communion... being in relationship is of the essence of things.[36]

---

[34] *Breath of Life*, 33, 51.
[35] Yves Congar, *I Believe in the Holy Spirit* (New York: Crossroad Publishing Company, 1997), II, 17.
[36] *Breath of Life*, 26.

In his writing, then, Edwards speaks of God's intimate relationship with humanity and all creation, and the ways in which humanity and creation are drawn into relationship with God, sharing in the divine communion. That God's Spirit implies relationships is critical to the development of one's spirituality. In Sacred Scripture, Paul described the Spirit of God as 'edifying', a term that means the Spirit is constructive, it builds relationships, builds community.[37]

In *Set Me Free*, I noted this Spirit-gifted communion of all creation in the unmistakable signs of the Spirit at work in the movements of our times: the movement towards justice and peace for the oppressed, the feminist movement seeking the full equality of women, and the ecological movement calling for a renewed relationship with the earth.[38] All of which signs involve relationships.

On feminism, I followed Denis Edwards, citing the work of Elizabeth Johnson. Johnson argued that our relationships suffer and creation is divided when an appreciation of God's giving Godself in Word and in Spirit is lost. She believed that the 'major taproot of the crisis' in both ecology and sexism is a 'hierarchical dualism' that divides reality into two separate and opposing spheres, assigning higher value to one over the other.

Johnson notes that 'humanity is detached from and more important than nature, man is separate from and more

---

[37] The term 'edifying' comes from the Latin word 'aedificare', literally 'to build'. I Corinthians 12:7 and 14:4.

[38] *Set Me Free*, 27.

valuable than woman, God is disconnected from the world, utterly and simply transcendent over it'.[39] She argues that 'these predicaments are intrinsically related to forgetting the Creator Spirit who pervades the world'. This was the starting point for Johnson's feminist theology, emphasising the fullness of humanity in all people.

In ecological theology and ecological practice, which Edwards developed from his initial theology of the Holy Spirit, we find the same emphasis on the inter-connectedness and inter-dependence of all creation. Relationships in creation exist in mutual relationship. Edwards argues that 'the theological insight that God's being is relational can provide a basis for a vision of the fundamental reality of the universe as relational'.[40] Thus he refers to 'Trinitarian relationships of mutual love'.

Pope Francis, too, stresses relationships in his encyclical on 'our common home', interpreting the creation accounts in the book of Genesis to suggest that human life is grounded in three fundamental and closely intertwined relationships: with God, with neighbour and with the earth itself.[41] The Pope writes that 'no creature is self-sufficient... creatures exist only in dependence on each other, to complete each other, in the service of each other'. This inter-dependence prompted Edwards' reference to 'Trinitarian relationships of mutual

---

[39] Elizabeth A. Johnson, *Woman, Earth and Creator Spirit* (New York: Paulist, 1993), 10-1. I developed Johnson's theology in *Set me Free*, 28-30.

[40] Denis Edwards, *Ecology at the Heart of Faith* (Maryknoll, NY: Orbis Books, 2006), 79-80.

[41] Francis, *Laudato Si'* (Strathfield NSW: St. Pauls Publications, 2015), #66.

love', the communion of all creation. God's vivifying Spirit in creation unites all creation in the communion of God's life.

Arguably, much of the present ecological crisis throughout the world – the exploitation of the earth's resources, the denudation of forests, the pollution of the earth and the atmosphere – has come about through a presumption that human beings dominate the rest of creation. The presumption has been that creation exists for the sake of humanity, the dualism described in Johnson's argument above. All creation is sacred, made so in the very moment of creation, confirmed by Jesus shedding his blood over the earth and the ever-present Spirit of love holding creation as one.

With Denis Edwards, I believe that God's gift of the Spirit, breathing in me and in all people, all creation, sustains us all in life. 'Wisdom... pervades and penetrates all things' (Wisdom 7:24). This is gift of God's very self, for God is a self-giving God. John of the Cross captured this in his poem *The Living Flame*,[42] cited earlier:

> Ah! Gentle and so loving
> you wake within me, proving
> that you are there in secret and alone;
> your fragrant breathing stills me,
> your grace, your glory fills me
> so tenderly your love becomes my own.

This gift of God's very self – God's Self-bestowal – doubtless inspired Rahner's writing on the Spirit, as well. In fact, in the chapter entitled *Reflections on the Experience of Grace* in

---

[42] *Centered on Love*, 22.

his *Theological Investigations*, Rahner goes further. He asks the question: 'Is it possible at all to experience grace in this life?'[43] He stresses that he is not talking about any pious feeling, but 'precisely the experience of grace – that is, a visitation of the Holy Spirit of the triune God.'

I found that I related quickly to Rahner's reflection. He distinguishes between our experience of spirit permeating or seasoning our earthly lives and everyday experience – as, for example, in our relationships and our enjoyment of art and music and creation – and the different experience of God's Spirit 'in its proper transcendence'. To capture this latter, Rahner asks questions to help the reader reflect on their personal experience:

Have we ever kept quiet, even though we wanted to defend ourselves when we had been unfairly treated? Have we ever forgiven someone even though we got no thanks and our silent forgiveness was taken for granted?... Have we ever decided on some course of action purely by the innermost judgment of our conscience, deep down where we can no longer tell or explain it to anyone, where one is quite alone?... Have we ever been good to someone who did not show the slightest sign of gratitude or comprehension and when we also were not rewarded by the feeling of having been 'selfless' or 'decent'?

Rahner argues that, if we are able to answer yes to these questions, then we have experienced something 'of eternity', an experience of the Spirit as 'more than merely part of

---

[43] Karl Rahner, *The Theology of the Spiritual Life*, volume III in *Theological Investigations* (Darton, Longman and Todd, 1967), 86-89.

this temporal world'. He calls such an experience 'a taste of pure Spirit'. I have noticed in my ministry as a spiritual director that many people do answer 'yes' to one or other of Rahner's questions, but it is usually a fairly tentative 'yes'. They say, understandably, that the experience is not what they imagined an experience of God would be like. There is no felt consolation. If anything, it feels more like loss, a kind-of dying.

I know the same in my own experience. Personally, I can recall an occasion when I was good to someone but received no gratitude, as in one of Rahner's questions. Though I was quite generous towards the other, that person seemed to have no appreciation of what I had done for them: there was no thankyou. At the time, I was well aware of the temptation to say something, at least to hint that some acknowledgment would be nice. Resisting that, I certainly experienced the empty feeling that Rahner mentions – it *is* a kind-of dying, dying to my need for affirmation.

Rahner insists that this is to experience 'pure Spirit'. Indeed, this apparent emptiness – that elsewhere he calls fullness – is to know God's Holy Spirit. I can add that, even while there is no felt consolation in such an experience, my relationship with the other person took a new turn: I noticed that I became more accepting of the other person, dare I say more loving. This is the surest indication for me that God's Spirit is at work. Earlier, Paul and Denis Edwards both reminded us that God's Spirit builds relationships.

Later, writing in the persona of Ignatius Loyola, Rahner speaks of his own experience as confirmation of his argument that one can and does experience God's Spirit:

All I am saying is this: I have experienced God, the nameless and unfathomable one, the silent and yet near one, in the trinity of his love for me... God himself, truly, God himself I experienced, and not simply human words about him...[44]

I would argue that Rahner is speaking of the same experience as John of the Cross, differing only in his different starting point and different terminology. Both call this 'dark' place a gift of grace.

The following chapter in which I consider the psychology of religious experience will shed more light on the experience described above as loss or dying.

---

[44] Karl Rahner, *Ignatius of Loyola Speaks*, trans. Annemarie S. Kidder (South Bend, IN: St Augustine's Press, 2013), 6, 9, 18.

# Love Sets Us Free

*The contemplative journey... is an
exercise of letting go of the false self,
a humbling process because it is the only self we know.*

THOMAS KEATING, LUIGI RULLA, GERALD MAY

In quite recent times, century 20/21, Thomas Keating was a Cistercian monk, one time Abbot of a large community in Massachusetts, USA. In 1981, he 'retired' to the community of Snowmass in Colorado. In the forty years there till his death in 2018, Keating established a thriving ministry in centering prayer. Of Keating's many published writings, most of which build on his experience of centering prayer, one *The Human Condition*[45] is a record of two occasional lectures which he was invited to give at Harvard Divinity School in 1997.

In *The Human Condition*, Keating's psychological insight, alongside his spiritual sensitivity, comes to the fore. He believed that 'psychology greatly supports religion and brings a certain clarity to areas of the human condition, especially the discovery of the unconscious'. Keating's lectures blended psychology and spirituality.

---

[45] Thomas Keating, *The Human Condition: Contemplation and Transformation* (New York: Paulist Press, 1999).

In the mixed bag of human experience, most people are aware of different attractions and repulsions in their inner world. The process of separating these various tendencies in ourselves is called discernment. Discernment is possible because we know that anything that is God-given will promote our true self and will challenge any falsity, whereas any spirits in us that are not of-God will promote untruth and unfreedom – and will even make them seem attractive!

If a person is honestly open to God's Spirit, anything not-of-God will be exposed – false images, hidden agendas, inner attachments or unfreedoms, any unconscious tendencies to control or manipulate God's work. These latter fall under what Keating refers to as one's 'false self' or self-created self. This self is false because 'its existence is based on its defending illusions'. The core illusion is that the false self imagines itself to be autonomous, the centre of its own meaning, effectively holding a person back from acceptance of God's love and loving relationships.

Thomas Keating calls the process of exposing one's false self 'divine therapy', a therapy for the 'tyranny of the false self'. He promotes such 'therapy' by the practice of centering prayer: 'the contemplative journey is an exercise of letting go of the false self, a humbling process because it is the only self we know'.[46]

Keating teaches that contemplative prayer and contemplative ministry serve to bring into our awareness any blocks or resistances to God's Spirit, enabling us to grow in freedom.

---

[46] *The Human Condition*, 19.

Keating says that 'if we don't allow the Spirit of God to address the deep levels of our attachments to ourselves and to our programs for happiness, we will pour into the world the negative elements of our self-centeredness...'[47] Conversely, when we *do* allow – and only when we allow – the Spirit of God to address the deep levels of our inner attachments, through contemplation, only then will we avoid pouring our self-centeredness into our world. These challenging words are reminiscent of Thomas Merton's strong statement:

> Those who attempt to act and do things for others ... without deepening their own self-understanding, freedom, integrity and capacity to love, will not have anything to give others. They will communicate to them nothing but the contagion of their own obsessions, their aggressiveness, their ego-centered ambitions and their delusions...[48]

Keating's starting point is the three essential biological needs all people are born with: needs for security and survival, power and control, affection and esteem. 'Without adequate fulfillment of these biological needs, we probably would not survive infancy.' He then traces normal human development, the development of consciousness, through childhood, adolescence, adulthood. Keating believes that Jesus' invitation to 'repent' is 'an invitation to grow up and become a fully mature human being who integrates the biological needs with the rational level of consciousness'. Whatever is not integrated remains in one's unconscious,

---

[47] *The Human Condition*, 36.
[48] Thomas Merton, *Contemplation in a World of Action* (University of Notre Dame Press, 1998), my earlier edition 1971.

resulting in the common human experience of mixed motivation. This explains Paul's oft-quoted description of his experience: 'I do not understand my own actions. For I do not do what I want, but I do the very thing I hate' (Romans 7:15).

Keating concludes that 'if we don't face the consequences of unconscious motivation – through a practice or discipline that opens us to the unconscious – then that motivation will secretly influence our decisions all through our lives'. At which point, Keating introduces the regular practice of contemplative centering prayer.

Centering prayer, as promoted by Thomas Keating, has a particular structure and a set of 'rules' to help stillness of mind and body. The technique usually suggests use of a mantra to help one remain focused. It is a contemplative prayer that listens and waits on God's word, as do many other forms of contemplative prayer, for example, the prayer described by John Chapman. As John pointed out, such prayer can seem quite empty, with little apparently happening in the prayer. We have said earlier that, in fact, much is happening below the surface: 'divine therapy' is at work, freeing us from unconscious levels of unfreedom. Keating notes here that John of the Cross' teaching on the experience of dark night corresponds to depth psychology:

> If psychologists and psychiatrists would be in dialogue with the insights of St John of the Cross and those who experience the dark nights, there could be a marvellous symbiosis of treatment.[49]

---

49 *The Human Condition*, 24.

Though Keating recommends the practice of centering prayer, I believe that any form of contemplative prayer serves the same purpose. For example, some people prefer the prayer of the breath, or others pray in their contemplation of a scriptural passage or some experience of nature.

Both John of the Cross and Thomas Keating see the desired fruit of contemplative prayer as growth in inner freedom, as gift of God. As we are freed of our false self – our inner places of unfreedom, even when unconscious – we become more open to God's love in our lives.

The psychology of human freedom and unfreedom has been studied by several authors. The approach and teaching of **Luigi Rulla** speaks accurately to my personal experience and my experience in ministry.

Luigi Rulla was more or less a contemporary of Thomas Keating, though it is doubtful that they ever met. Rulla, a Jesuit priest, an anthropologist and a psychologist, headed the Institute of Psychology at the Gregorian University in Rome from 1971 till his death in 2002. I discuss aspects of Rulla's teaching that seem relevant to my discussion of Thomas Keating.

Though all people have been gifted with freedom, it is a freedom rarely fully experienced, as Paul reminded us in the statement I have already referred to:

> I do not understand my own actions. For I do not do what I want, but I do the very thing I hate... I do not do the good I want, but the evil I do not want is what I do. (Romans 7:15)

Rulla used the terminology of *essential* freedom and *effective* freedom. We are created free: to be human is to be free, but we know from our experience that our freedom is limited. Rulla's research studied effective freedom, concluding that 'psychodynamic factors may influence the degree of freedom with which the individual is disposed to the action of grace'.

Traditional teaching in spirituality acknowledges the experience of limited freedom, often describing the experience in terms of our self-created image of ourselves. As Keating emphasised, such self-created images have no basis in reality, no matter how virtuous they may appear or how much time and energy has gone into cultivating them.

As discussed in my book *Set me Free*, the term *attachments* is commonly used to describe those areas of one's inner life that are not free. This is the term used by John of the Cross, Teresa of Avila, Ignatius Loyola and others.

I emphasise that attachments are experiences of unfreedom or limited freedom in our inner life. Such attachments in our inner life show themselves in emotional habits of behaviour. Even though our inner unfreedoms are unconscious, our patterns of behaviour are often the first indication of their presence. But these places of unfreedom and their consequent behavioural patterns are usually well entrenched. Even with some awareness, only cooperation with the grace of God makes growth in inner freedom possible.

Rulla introduces a rather nuanced use of the terminology of human 'needs'. Whereas Keating spoke of basic biological needs for security, control, and affection, Rulla sees human needs as 'innate tendencies to act in certain ways.'[50] When I always react in a certain way to others' criticism, for example, it is as though I 'need' to react, maybe because I am already low on self-esteem. These are the psychodynamic factors referred to above. Rulla used more technical terminology when he listed, for example, the need for autonomy, the need for succorance (for constant assurance or affirmation), the need for dominance, the need for achievement, etc. – twenty-two needs in all, in some sense all found in all people, but in different need strengths and need patterns. All our needs flow from early childhood experience, as a child manages to cope with a less-than-perfect world. Seeing 'needs' in this sense helps me to understand our limited freedom. If a person has an unconscious need for succorance, for example, much of their behaviour and their decision-making will be for the sake of affirmation. The need will always want to be met.

This understanding has helped me also to recognise that a person's vulnerability to the temptation of spirits not-of-God flows from this place of limited freedom. Spirits not-of-God are subtle enough to appeal to a person's unconscious needs. Any course of action that serves to feed an inner need effectively hinders growth and hinders relationship with God. When this happens, self-transcendence – rising above one's need – is highly unlikely:

> Depth psychology shows that it is possible for people to desire and to profess the ideals of Christ, while, without

---

[50] Luigi Rulla, *Anthropology of the Christian Vocation* (Rome: Gregorian University Press, 1986). 133 & App. B.

being aware of this, they are also driven by subconscious needs which cannot be reconciled with these ideals. Therefore, the individual is *inconsistent* in the sense that they are moved simultaneously by two opposed forces: one being the ideals which they consciously desire and the judgment of values which they make, the other being the deep-lying needs by which they are subconsciously driven.[51]

Examples of this inconsistency are Paul's 'I do not do what I want to do' and Augustine's 'Lord, make me chaste, but not yet'.[52]

This approach is supported also by **Gerald May**. A psychiatrist and a spiritual director, May was based at the Shalem Institute in Washington DC until his death in 2005. May, too, blended his psychological and spiritual experience. His book *Will and Spirit*, for example, is subtitled *A Contemplative Psychology*.[53]

Gerald May believed that we do not come to any relationship in our lives utterly freely. Even in our relationship with God, we necessarily bring some level of self-interest or possessiveness, in most instances, quite unconsciously.

Like Keating and Rulla, May believes that we are essentially free people, created free: 'We must claim the freedom we have

---

[51] Rulla, 'The Discernment of Spirits and Christian Anthropology,' *Gregorianum* 59, no. 3 (1978): 546.

[52] For other examples, see Brian Gallagher, *God's Foolishness* (Bayswater Vic: Coventry Press, 2020), 48-51.

[53] *Will and Spirit: A Contemplative Psychology*, HarperOne, 1987.

been given. To do otherwise would devalue our humanity'.[54] Instead of Rulla's terminology of 'inner needs', May uses the psychological term 'addiction' to describe our places of unfreedom:

> Working against (our freedom) is the powerful force of addiction. Psychologically, addiction uses up desire... Spiritually, addiction is a deep-seated form of idolatry. The objects of our addictions become our false gods... To define it directly, addiction is a state of compulsion, obsession or preoccupation that enslaves a person's will and desire.[55]

Precisely because we are created free, we believe that God desires freedom for all and always works towards freedom for God's people. We aspire to this freedom and know that, with grace, it is within reach. At the same time, cooperation with this grace of God can be quite demanding. May believes it 'may be the greatest struggle any human being can face, and it may call forth the greatest courage and dedication...'[56] May summarises that 'the joy and beauty of freedom and love must be bought with pain'.[57]

The pain in this growth has already been described by John of the Cross' teaching on dark night. May knew John of the Cross well, evidenced by his fine study *The Dark Night of the Soul*. This is his summation of John's teaching:

---

[54] Gerald G May, *Care of Mind, Care of Spirit* (San Francisco, CA: Harper & Row, 1982), 63.
[55] Gerald G May, *Addiction and Grace* (San Francisco, CA: HarperSanFrancisco, 1988), 13-4.
[56] *Addiction and Grace*, 19.
[57] *Addiction and Grace*, 117.

Regardless of when and how it happens, the dark night of the soul is the transition from bondage to freedom in prayer and in every other aspect of life... we find an ever-increasing freedom to be who we really are in an identity that is continually emerging and never defined.[58]

(The dark night) is the secret way in which God not only liberates us from our attachments and idolatries, but also brings us to the realisation of our true nature. The night is the means by which we find our heart's desire, our freedom for love.[59]

All of these writers teach that growth in inner freedom comes as gift of God, described with different emphases by John of the Cross, Karl Rahner, Thomas Keating and Gerald May.

---

[58] Gerald G May, *The Dark Night of the Soul* (San Francisco, CA: HarperSanFrancisco, 2004), 132-3.
[59] *The Dark Night of the Soul*, 67.

# Conclusion

'In this is love: not that we loved God, but that God loved us...
We love because God first loved us' (1 John 4:10, 19). John's
insistence that God first loved us is the foundation of all
spirituality. Only when we know that love in our hearts –
and know it because we have experienced it – are we able to
live truly happy lives. All of the women and men named in
this book knew well the love of God poured into their hearts
by the Holy Spirit given to them. All knew that there is no
greater love than that.

We do not necessarily expect to experience God's personal
love as dramatically and powerfully as did John of the Cross,
for example: 'you looked with love upon me'. Love is gift.
We allow the giver to determine when and how the love is
given. Our role is to receive, humbly and gratefully, beautifully
captured by Francis de Sales' image of the baby at her
mother's breast. At one point, John of the Cross wrote that
'contemplation is to receive'. I see Mary, the womb of God,
as the model of a contemplative life-style: Mary received the
Word of God, literally in her womb and symbolically in her
whole being. Mary's response to the angel 'let it be done to
me' became joyful praise of God: 'my soul magnifies the Lord
and my spirit rejoices in God my saviour'. My encouragement
to a contemplative way of praying and living flows from this.

All of the women and men named in this book lived
such lives. All found that God's personal love for them

sustained them through life. This is particularly evident in the experiences of God's apparent absence, highlighted by William of St Thierry, John of the Cross and John Chapman, and implied by Karl Rahner. It is a sobering reminder that God's presence and God's care for us is not determined by our feeling that presence. Sometimes all we have is our faith and our desire for God. Our desire for God, in some sense, is enough: desire for God is a place of God already.

Finally, all the women and men in this book were committed to an honest response to God's love in the way they lived their own lives. All were loving people – we love because God first loved us. Indeed, 'your love becomes my own'. All were prayerful people, committed to deepening their own personal relationship with God. And all were self-giving people – they committed their lives for the sake of other people, whether in face-to-face ministry, as in Bill Connolly, Francis de Sales, Luigi Rulla and Gerald May, in the ministry of writing to spread God's word, notably in Marjorie Flower, Denis Edwards, Karl Rahner and John of the Cross, or in the ministry of prayer and penance, explicitly so in the monks and in Julian of Norwich. Spirituality has to be lived, shared, for the good of all God's people.

## Recommended Reading

John of the Cross, *Centered on Love: the Poems of St John of the Cross* Translated by Marjorie Flower ocd (Varroville NSW: Carmelite Nuns, 1983, reprinted 2002).

Thomas Keating, *The Human Condition: Contemplation and Transformation*(New York: Paulist Press, 1999).

Gerald G May, *The Dark Night of the Soul* (San Francisco, CA: HarperSanFrancisco, 2004).